7,36

O9-BTJ-974

A Guide for Using

Bud, Not Buddy

in the Classroom

Based on the book written by Christopher Paul Curtis

*This guide written by **Sarah Kartchner Clark, M.A.***

Teacher Created Materials, Inc.
6421 Industry Way
Westminster, CA 92683
www.teachercreated.com
©2001 Teacher Created Materials
Made in U.S.A.
ISBN 0-7439-3153-x

Edited by
Eric Migliaccio

Illustrated by
Bruce Hedges

Cover Art by
Bruce Hedges

The classroom teacher may reproduce copies of materials in this book for classroom use only. The reproduction of any part for an entire school or school system is strictly prohibited. No part of this publication may be transmitted, stored, or recorded in any form without written permission from the publisher.

Table of Contents

Introduction

Literature opens the door to magical new worlds. Historical fiction is an engaging genre of literature that is quick to read, and yet leaves a lasting impression. Historical fiction also teaches us of our past and of the way things were. Within the pages of a story are words, vocabulary, and characters that can inspire us to achieve our highest ideals. We can turn to stories for companionship, recreation, comfort, and guidance.

By engaging our imaginations and emotions, stories let us learn about people we may never meet and explore places to which we may never go. The best stories also help us discover more about ourselves. Like a good friend, a good story touches and enriches our lives forever.

In *Literature Units,* great care has been taken to select books that are sure to become good friends!

Teachers who use this literature unit will find the following features to supplement their own valuable ideas:

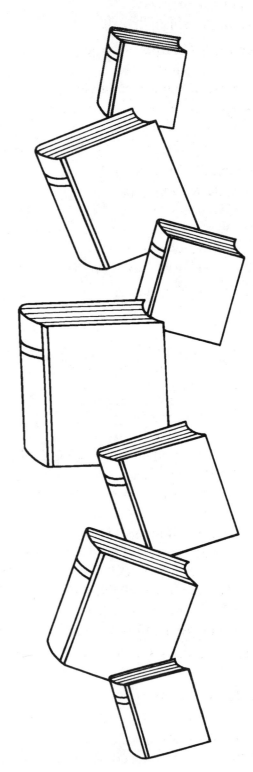

- Sample Lesson Plans
- Pre-Reading Activities
- A Biographical Sketch and Picture of the Author
- A Book Summary
- Vocabulary Lists and Suggested Vocabulary Activities
- Chapters grouped for study with each section including:
  —quizzes
  —hands-on projects
  —cooperative learning activities
  —cross-curriculum connections
  —extensions into the reader's own life
- Post-reading Activities
- Research Ideas
- Book Report Ideas
- Culminating Activities
- Three Different Options for Unit Tests
- Bibliography of Related Reading
- Answer Key

Using this unit as part of your teaching strategy can help you show your students how reading can touch their lives in wondrous ways.

Sample Lesson Plans

Each of the lessons suggested below can take from one to several days to complete.

Lesson 1

- Introduce and complete some or all of the pre-reading activities. (page 5)
- Read "About the Author" with your students. (page 6)
- Introduce the vocabulary list for chapters 1–3. (page 8)

Lesson 2

- Read chapters 1–3 of *Bud, Not Buddy*. As you read, place the vocabulary words in the context of the story and discuss their meanings.
- Choose a vocabulary activity. (page 9)
- Follow the directions to make "Helping-People Pamphlets." (page 11)
- Work in groups to create a newspaper from the 1930s. (page 12)
- Do the math problems relating to the Depression. (page 13)
- Complete the "If I Were Bud . . ." activities. (page 14)
- Administer the section 1 quiz. (page 10)
- Introduce the vocabulary list for chapters 4–8. (page 8)

Lesson 3

- Read chapters 4–8 of *Bud, Not Buddy*. As you read, place the vocabulary words in the context of the story and discuss their meanings.
- Choose a vocabulary activity. (page 9)
- Create a Hooverville diorama. (page 16)
- Participate in a literature discussion group about the reading thus far. (page 17)
- Complete the "Railroad Ties" page and learn about youngsters who rode the rails. (page 18)
- Compare and contrast the 1930s to today. (page 19)
- Administer the section 2 quiz. (page 15)
- Introduce the vocabulary list for chapters 9–11. (page 8)

Lesson 4

- Read chapters 9–11 of *Bud, Not Buddy*. As you read, place the vocabulary words in the context of the story and discuss their meanings.
- Choose a vocabulary activity. (page 9)
- Design a stained art painting and a diamonte poem on a scene from the book. (page 21)
- Complete the "Dicey Descriptions" to review and learn the use of adjectives. (page 22)
- Learn the meaning and importance of literary devices used in writing. (page 23)
- Write a fable. (page 24)
- Administer the section 3 quiz. (page 20)
- Introduce the vocabulary list for chapters 12–14. (page 8)

Lesson 5

- Read chapters 12–14 of *Bud, Not Buddy*. As you read, place the vocabulary words in the context of the story and discuss their meanings.
- Choose a vocabulary activity. (page 9)
- Create a home movie on the history of communications. (page 26)
- Hold a class debate on labor unions. (page 27)
- Write a message, using Morse code. (page 28)
- Learn the meaning and use of euphemisms. (page 29)
- Administer the section 4 quiz. (page 25)
- Introduce the vocabulary list for chapters 15–19. (page 8)

Lesson 6

- Read chapters 15–19 of *Bud, Not Buddy*. As you read, place the vocabulary words in the context of the story and discuss their meanings.
- Choose a vocabulary activity. (page 9)
- Design a poster for Bud's opening night. (page 31)
- Map the places that the Dusky Devastators traveled during the Depression. (page 32)
- Answer graphing questions, using a graph on labor union membership. (page 33)
- Write an historical fiction story, using friends and family members as characters. (page 34)
- Administer the section 5 quiz. (page 30)

Lesson 7

- Assign post-reading activities. (pages 35–37)
- Begin work on culminating activities. (pages 38–42)

Lesson 8

- Administer Unit Tests 1, 2, and/or 3. (pages 43–45)
- Provide a list of related reading materials for your students. (page 46)

Before the Book

Before students begin reading *Bud, Not Buddy*, have them participate in some pre-reading activities to stimulate interest and enhance their comprehension of short stories.

1. *Bud, Not Buddy* has a variety of themes prevalent throughout the story. Some of these themes are friendship, family relationships, racism, hope, survival, and endurance. Set up a book display of children's books that deal with these themes. Allow students time to browse and read some of these stories. Ask students to write down observations they have about these themes.

2. Show a picture of Christopher Paul Curtis and look up an interview of him on the Internet. (See the bibliography on page 46 for Web sites and pages.) Explain that you will be reading a book written by him. Explain that this is Christopher Paul Curtis' second book. Both of his books have been awarded the Newbery Medal. For more information on the Newbery Medal, look up the Official Web site on the Internet.

3. Read about Christopher Paul Curtis (page 6). Review some aspects of his life with the students. Discuss the following questions:

   • Where did Christopher Paul Curtis get information for this book?

   • What would it be like to work in a factory for thirteen years?

   • Who inspired Christopher Paul Curtis to begin writing books?

   • What do you think his story will be about?

   • Who were the important individuals that two characters are based on?

   • How did his life help him write stories?

   • Have you ever used incidents in your life to write a story?

4. Distribute copies of *Bud, Not Buddy*. Have students look at the cover and title. Have students make predictions about what they think the story is about. Ask students if this book looks or sounds like any other books they have previously read.

5. The events in *Bud, Not Buddy* take place during the 1930s and the Depression. Invite to your classroom people who lived during that time period. Allow time for students to ask questions about what it was like to live then. Some questions might include: What did families do for fun? What was the music like? How is life different for kids now? What was the Depression? What did people do if they lost their job? What did the government do to help? Encourage guests to bring any pictures they have of that time in their life.

6. Read a part of the first chapter to students. Based on these few paragraphs, work together as a class to map out what they think will happen in this story. This is a prediction story map. Draw this map on a large piece of poster paper. Post this somewhere in the classroom for students to review as they read. What parts of the prediction were accurate, which parts were inaccurate?

7. Locate on a map where Flint, Michigan is. See the bibliography at the back of the unit for a web site that has information on what life was like during the Depression in Flint, Michigan.

8. Discuss with the class the definition of an orphan. What is a "Home"? How would it feel to be in a "Home"? Ask students to share their feelings about what it would be like to be an orphan. Some questions you could ask are: What would some of the hardships be? How would you be able to cope? What types of things does Bud have to do without because he has no parents?

About the Author

Christopher Paul Curtis—who was born in Flint, Michigan—currently lives in Windsor, Ontario, Canada, with his wife, Kaysandra, and their two children, Steven and Cydney. Hobbies that Curtis enjoys are playing basketball, collecting old record albums, and writing. It is this last hobby that has earned him many awards and accolades.

After attending the University of Michigan, Curtis worked for 13 years as a factory worker at the Fisher Body plant in Flint, Michigan. Other jobs he has had include being a maintenance man, campaign worker, customer service representative, warehouse clerk, and purchasing clerk.

Curtis, who spent many of his breaks at the factory writing, is actually a relative newcomer to the literary world. His first book, entitled *The Watsons Go to Birmingham—1963*, was published in 1995; and *Bud, Not Buddy* is his second. While Curtis' body of work is small, the amount of success and recognition he has received has been anything but. *The Watsons Go to Birmingham—1963* was a Newbery Honor book, and *Bud, Not Buddy* was the winner of the Newbery Medal of Honor. Also, both books have won the Coretta Scott King Award.

Curtis submitted his first story to the Delacorte's First Young Adult Novel Contest. This was the beginning of his writing success. Writing is a relaxing and peaceful activity for Curtis and he encourages others to write as well. He suggests that authors spend time each day practicing their craft. Writing takes time and effort. Curtis suggests that young authors keep working to improve and be patient as stories develop.

The biggest influence for Curtis while growing up was his parents, who were strict and structured. Family has played an important role in Curtis' work; in fact, two of the characters in *Bud, Not Buddy* are patterned after his grandfathers Earl "Lefty" Lewis and Herman E. Curtis, and many of the other characters in his books are based on friends or members of his family. Part of Curtis' inspiration for writing *Bud, Not Buddy* came from a family reunion he attended. There he learned about his grandfather and began to ask questions and take notes about his grandfather's life.

Though he wasn't encouraged to do much creative writing in school as a child, Curtis always enjoyed reading and writing. He was taught more about the grammar and structure of writing. He attributes his ability to complete his first novel to his wife, who encouraged him to take a year off to write. He did, and the results were rewarding.

Curtis never intended to write books for young adults. That is just the category where his books were placed. However, he does love the honesty and forthrightness of children. He believes that they have an uncanny ability to discern the truth.

Curtis also has a love for learning. Many of his ideas about labor unions came from research and information gathered when learning about the strikes and labor union issues that took place at the plant where he worked. He asked questions, and he learned about the Depression. Taking notes of facts and historical details and then weaving them into his stories brings history to life in Curtis' books and helps them feel real and alive.

Bud, Not Buddy

by Christopher Paul Curtis

(Delacorte Press, 1999)

(Available in Canada, Doubleday Dell Seal; UK, Bantam Doubleday Dell; and Australia, Transworld.)

Bud, Not Buddy is the story of a 10-year-old boy who was orphaned at the age of six. The setting of the story is the Depression of the 1930s. The story opens with Bud in an orphanage. He is soon thereafter sent to a home to live with a family. This is not a good thing for Bud, as the family is mean and abusive. Bud gets his revenge on the family, and the story of his will to survive and succeed begins.

On the run, Bud carries in a cardboard suitcase his most prized possessions, among which are a few rocks with numbers written on them and several flyers advertising a band called Herman E. Calloway and the Dusky Devastators. Bud is not sure what these items mean, but he remembers that both the rocks and the flyers held some special significance to his mother. While attempting to figure out the meaning of these items, Bud becomes convinced that the man in each of these flyers—Herman E. Calloway—is his father. Bud's story is his adventure of finding Mr. Calloway.

Some of the events that happen along the way include staying at a Hooverville, trying to catch a train; running from the foster home; walking to Grand Rapids, Michigan; catching a ride from a Railroad Union Leader; and being included in a make-believe family in order to get a bowl of oatmeal. His will to survive and succeed keeps Bud moving.

As a means to survive, Bud constructs a list of rules "for Having a Funner Life and Make a Better Liar Out of Yourself." Rules from this list are woven through each chapter of the book. Bud meets up with enemies and friends throughout the book. Some of the enemies are characters, while others are the dictates of his environment. Living during the Depression lends itself to many struggles and obstacles.

Bud visits a Hooverville in anticipation of catching a train to get out of Flint. It is here that he kisses a girl for the first time. Bud often thinks of this girl after his experience of talking to her and learning about life. It is through her that he learns that his Momma will always be inside of him.

Bud misses the train and heads for Grand Rapids, Michigan. He determines once again to find Herman E. Calloway, the man he believes is his father. It is at this point in the story that he meets up with Lefty Lewis. Lefty convinces Bud to get in his car. Lefty brings Bud home to his daughter's house for a good night's rest and a delicious breakfast.

Lewis sends a telegraph to Calloway telling him that he has his son and will bring him back. Bud is dropped off at Calloway's home where he is greeted with questions and suspicion, yet is invited to stay. Surrounded by the band members and Miss Thomas, Bud eats his first meal at a restaurant. Overcome by emotion, Bud cries. On the next trip, Bud rides home with Mr. Calloway. After the performance, Mr. Calloway picks up a rock and scribbles on it the city and numbers just like all the rocks that Bud has been carrying in his suitcase. As more details unfold, Mr. Calloway, Miss Thomas, and the band members realize that Bud is indeed related to Mr. Calloway, but not in the way that Bud thinks.

Themes presented in the book include survival, hope, family, friendship, racism, and the Depression. This story ends on a happy note with Bud receiving his first instrument—an alto sax—from the band members. Bud begins his new life, learning about music, family, and the meaning of life.

Vocabulary Lists

On this page are vocabulary lists that correspond to each section of *Bud, Not Buddy*. Vocabulary activity ideas can be found on page 9.

Section 1 (Chapters 1–3)

depression	icebox	paddled
beloved	padlock	glum
conscience	simmered	engagement
lavatory	vermin	luxurious
locomotive	urchins	provoked
ilk	ingratitude	plagues
brute	foster	

Section 2 (Chapters 4–8)

lam	valve	wiry
telegraph	matrimonial	Hooverville
strap	radiating	radiating
crapper	gait	smack
upside	mission	cellar
whiff	hoodlum	busting
tetters	britches	

Section 3 (Chapters 9–11)

devoured	dangling	paltry
ventriloquists	belt (verb)	knickers
gory	wrestled	puny
piped	slew	tatters
crick	glimpse	scrawny
rustle	spitting image	undergo
bum-rush		

Section 4 (Chapters 12–14)

sully	shunned	scours up
resourceful	coot	offense
alias	meddling	swopped
plug (verb)	prying	palest
ethyl	gig	rassle
moldering	craws	ratted
scamp	acquaintance	

Section 5 (Chapters 15–19)

embouchure	dinky	spirit
prodigy	insinuating	scales
scamp	merchandise	ornery
godsend	reed	curtsy
copacetic	outhouses	
slacking	pulse	

Vocabulary Activities

Help your students to learn and retain the necessary vocabulary from *Bud, Not Buddy* by providing them with interesting vocabulary activities.

Context Clues

Have students look up each vocabulary word in the context it was written. Using the context clues, have students write what they think the words mean. Then, using a dictionary, have students look up each word and see if the definition they wrote matches the definition in the dictionary. Use an online dictionary, if desired.

Substitutions

Have students look up each vocabulary word in the book. They should then rewrite the sentence in which the vocabulary word is found but insert a synonym in place of the vocabulary word. Have students share their sentences with each other. See if they can figure out the original vocabulary word that was used in each sentence.

Individual Activities

Students can do one of the following activities individually: create word searches or crossword puzzles, use each vocabulary word in a story, make their own dictionary/thesaurus using vocabulary words, make a part-of-speech chart categorizing the vocabulary words, and/or write the words in alphabetical order.

Once Upon a Time . . .

Have students select 10 words from the vocabulary lists. Have students write a fictional story that uses the words somewhere in the story. Instruct students to underline each word. Encourage students to double-check the definitions and the proper use of each vocabulary word.

Speaking of Parts

Have students make a chart that includes headings such as nouns, verbs, adverbs, adjectives, pronouns, etc. Instruct students to place each vocabulary word under the correct heading. Students may then check their chart by looking each vocabulary word up in the dictionary and finding the part of speech listed. (Be sure to remind students that the first part of speech listed under each definition may not be the part of speech for the vocabulary word. Some other forms of the word are usually listed at the end of the definition with the corresponding part of speech.)

The Real World

Using magazines or newspapers, have students locate and highlight each vocabulary word being used. Students may also look (or listen) for these vocabulary words being used in brochures, junk mail, on the backs of cereal boxes, on the radio, or in songs. Have students bring samples of the vocabulary words being used. Give students points for each sample they are able to find. Create a bulletin board to post and display samples of vocabulary words being used. (Note: Some of the vocabulary words are words that were used during the 1930s, the time period in which the book is written. Give students double points for locating words designated ahead of time as challenging words to find.)

Quiz Time

Answer the following questions about *Bud, Not Buddy*.

1. On the back of this paper, write a one-paragraph summary of chapters 1–3. Then complete the rest of the questions on this page.

2. Where is Bud sent to from the orphanage? _____

   _____

3. What did Todd shove up Bud's nose? What was Bud's reaction to this? _____

   _____

4. What did Todd's mother do when she came into the room and found the two boys fighting? _____

   _____

5. Where did Bud get sent to sleep for the night? _____

6. What is Bud afraid of in the shed? _____

   _____

7. What did the vampire bat end up being? What really happens to Bud when he feels like someone stuck a red-hot nail into his left cheek? _____

   _____

8. How does Bud escape from the shed? _____

   _____

   _____

9. What do rules #3, #118, and #328 say? _____

   _____

   _____

   _____

   _____

10. What were the flyers in Bud's suitcase advertising? _____

    _____

    _____

Helping-People Pamphlets

There were many programs set up during the Depression by President Roosevelt and his "New Deal." These programs were meant to help individuals in need. Select one of the programs listed below and use the Internet, encyclopedias, and/or books to research it. You may also gather information from a family member or neighbor that lived during that time. Once you have gathered information, create a pamphlet or brochure advertising the agency you have researched. How is this agency helpful? Is it still in place today?

Programs of the New Deal

- AAA
- CCC
- FERA
- FDIC
- FLSA
- FSA
- HOLC

- NLRB
- NRA
- NYA
- SEC
- Social Security
- TVA
- WPA

(See *Bibliography* for more information on the New Deal and these programs.)

Materials

Items for decoration, including . . .

- colored paper
- construction paper
- scissors

- pencils
- magazines
- markers

- colored pencils
- stickers

Directions

1. Place the construction paper with the short side at the top. Fold colored paper in thirds. Turn paper sideways, so that the long side of the pamphlet is vertical.

2. Design the layout for your pamphlet. Where will the title go? What colors and decorations will make the pamphlet look attractive? Draw illustrations or cut pictures from magazines.

3. State the problem that will be addressed by the New Deal program and how the program will help alleviate that problem. Be sure to keep in mind letter size and color to attract the reader's attention. Also, be sure to include accurate, factual, and useful information about the agency you are advertising.

4. Use markers, colored pencils, stickers, pictures from magazines, etc., to decorate your pamphlet.

1930s Newspaper

Research the time period of the Great Depression and create a newspaper from that time. You will be assigned to a group of four or five students and given a specific job on the newspaper staff. The role and role descriptions are listed below.

☞ Editorials/Editorial Cartoons

You are the editor of the newspaper. It is your job to write an editorial about an event that is going on during the Depression. Research facts, news, and information of this time period. Using persuasive writing, write an editorial essay to include in the newspaper. Before writing an editorial, determine your opinion on the issue you will be researching. Once you have written your opinion, change it to a thesis statement. For example, your opinion might be, "I think the United States government should be more involved in helping people." A thesis statement can then read, "The United States government must offer more assistance to the American people." An editorial states the thesis statement at the beginning, and then supplies at least three statements that support the thesis. Illustrate an editorial cartoon to go along with your editorial. Look at samples of editorials and editorial cartoons in magazines or newspapers.

☞ News and Events of the 1930s

This reporter will be researching and locating news and current events of the 1930s. After gathering research, write a newspaper article about your information. Remember to answer the six main questions: who, what, where, why, when, and how. Write the article in the present tense, as if it were the 1930s now. Draw an illustration to go with your article.

☞ Entertainment/Jazz/Swing/Music

This reporter will be searching for information on entertainment and music of the 1930s. What did kids do for fun? What did adults do? What was the music like during this time? Write an article about the entertainment of this time, and make a listing of entertainment and events that would be happening during the 1930s.

☞ Technology of the 1930s

What were the inventions of this time period? What was the technology news of this decade? How did these inventions change people's lives? As a reporter, write an article about the new and upcoming inventions of the 1930s. Read the technology section of your local newspaper to get ideas on how to write about this news. Draw an illustration or print one off the Internet.

☞ Newspaper Format

Once each of the reporters in your group have gathered the research and written the articles, determine the format for your group newspaper. Work together to determine the headlines. What will go on the front page? Which illustrations will attract readers to read the paper? What will the name of your newspaper be? Add finishing touches with classifieds, advertisements, crossword puzzles, etc., as desired.

Depression Story Problems

All of the imaginary story problems on this page are written about the Depression time period. It should be noted that the figures are not exact. Three different ways to use this page are described here.

◆ Write a problem on the chalkboard each day for students to solve as they come into the classroom.

◆ Copy this page and cut along the dotted lines. Place the problems in a paper bag and have each student draw one problem to solve.

◆ Use these problems at a math center in your classroom.

1. Unemployment rose from two million in 1929 to 12 million by 1933. What is the difference between the two unemployment figures?

2. If a shack built in a Hooverville is three feet long and five feet wide, what is the area of the shack?

3. Four hundred miles of telegraph wires were built along the railroad in eight years. Approximately how many miles of telegraph wires were put up each year?

4. In 1931 approximately eight million people lost their jobs and became unemployed. By 1932, 12 million people were without jobs. How many more people lost their jobs in 1932?

5. The price of flour in 1933 was 20¢ for five pounds. If the price of flour today is 40¢ per pound, what is the percent of increase?

$$\frac{\text{price today} - 1933 \text{ price}}{1933 \text{ price}} \times 100 = \frac{\text{percent of}}{\text{increase}}$$

6. A small fraction of the children were well nourished during the Depression. If the fraction were ⅕, what would the percentage of well nourished children be?

7. If unemployment during the Depression was around four million in 1930, 12 million in 1932, around 13 million in 1933, and 11 million in 1934, what was the average number of unemployed during those four years?

8. If the orphanages throughout the country found homes for 232 children in 1932, 143 in 1933, and 102 in 1934, what is the total number of children placed in foster care during those three years?

9. A local grocer was donating apples to 16 men to sell on the street. There was a total of 715 pounds to give away. About how many pounds did each man get to sell?

10. There were 4,431 boys and 5,672 girls attending school in Walker County during 1934. Round the number of boys and the number of girls attending school to the nearest thousand.

11. One-eighth of the vegetables donated to the local mission came from farms in the east. Five-eights came from farms in the west. Two-eighths of the vegetables came from the state government. What fraction of the total amount of vegetables was donated by the farms?

12. In the United States, 300,000 immigrants arrived annually, even though there was a Depression going on. At that rate, how many people came in five years?

If I Were Bud . . .

Understanding and thinking like the main character is important when reading stories. Some characters are easy to relate to, while others are more difficult to understand. What are your thoughts about Bud? Does he make a lot of the same decisions that you would? What would you do differently? How is his life different than yours. Select three or more of the following activities to complete. You will be sharing your work with a small group of students.

=========================== **Activities** ===========================

1. Write a diary entry as if you were Bud. Select an event from your own life to write about in this diary as though you were Bud writing it. Be sure to include the date and the location.

2. Write a letter from Bud to one of the following people: his mother, Bugs, Herman C. Calloway, the Amos family, the kids at the orphanage, Deza, Mrs. Sleet, Miss Hill, Miss Thomas, or the jazz band. What would he tell them? In his letter, have him describe his surroundings and his feelings.

3. Make a time line with small pictures illustrating Bud's adventure in search of his father. Be sure to list the events in chronological order. Add tidbits of information next to each event listed.

4. Turn Bud's adventure into a picture book for little children. Include some details from your own life into the story. Write this in the form of a children's book with illustrations and a title page. What will the title of your story be?

5. Draw a Venn diagram on the back of this paper and compare and contrast yourself with Bud. In what ways are you similar? In what ways are you different? Don't forget to compare and contrast such things as surroundings, family, personality, beliefs, characteristics, and experiences.

6. Bud has had many different challenges in his life. Make a list of the setbacks that Bud has had thus far in the book. Make a list of challenges or setbacks you have had in your life. What strategies does Bud use to overcome his trials. What things have you done to meet your challenges? What things have you found helpful as you overcome trials?

7. Bud makes a list of rules that he uses in his life. Which rules do you think are accurate, and which ones do you think are foolish? What rules do you have in your life? Make a list of rules that have helped you in your life. Share your list with family members and classmates. See if there are any more you could add to the list.

8. Add a new character to *Bud, Not Buddy*. How would Bud interact with this character? Would he like the character? Write in detail about an incident including Bud and the character you have created.

9. Create a readers' theater script about an event from the section you have just read. Enlist the help of some other students and present the reader's theater to the class. You play the role of Bud. How does he sound? What kind of expressions does he use? What is his personality like?

10. Make a poster advertising why Bud would be a great child to adopt. What are his strong points? How would he add to a family? Remember to consider letter size, colors, design, and information displayed; make your poster look professional.

Quiz Time

Answer the following questions about *Bud, Not Buddy*.

1. On the back of this paper, write a one-paragraph summary of chapters 4–8. Then complete the rest of the questions on this page.

2. How did Bud get revenge on the Amos family? _____
   _____
   _____

3. What happened to Miss Hill, the librarian?_____
   _____
   _____

4. What did Momma and her dad get in a fight about when she got her picture taken on the miniature horse? _____
   _____
   _____

5. What were the four things Momma used to always talk to Bud about?_____
   _____
   _____
   _____

6. Bud was late for breakfast at the Mission. He got to eat anyway. How? What did he get sprinkled on his oatmeal? _____
   _____
   _____

7. Who is Deza Malone? What does Bud do for the first time with Deza?_____
   _____
   _____

8. What was the town "Hooperville" like? _____
   _____
   _____

9. What happens when Bud tries to catch the train with Bugs? _____
   _____
   _____

10. What does Bud notice about the names "Calloway" and "Caldwell"?_____
   _____

Create a Hooverville

During the Great Depression, many families lost their homes because they could not pay their mortgages. These families had no choice but to build shelters out of wood scraps and cardboard. Families grouped together to form what was called a "Hooverville." These makeshift towns were named after President Hoover, who was blamed for the problems brought on by the Depression. Bud and Bugs are trying to find a town called "Hooperville," when they come across a Hooverville. They quickly learn about these mini-cities.

Materials

- shoebox
- crayons/paints
- scissors

- glue
- tape

- materials to use for scenery (e.g., cardboard, construction paper, fabric, foil, magazine pictures, tissue paper, etc.)

Directions

1. Take the top off the shoebox. Cut a hole along one side, or on one end of the shoebox.

2. On a separate piece of paper, draw a sketch of what your Hooverville will look like. Use the sketch to create your Hooverville scene. Build a scene inside the box (facing the hole). Place figures or objects that are most important near the front. Glue scenery to the back and sides of the box.

3. Add people or animals to the Hooverville to make it look realistic. In *Bud, Not Buddy*, we learn that there were fires for cooking and washing clothes, tin cans for scooping and carrying things, and cardboard boxes for shelter.

4. Cut a slit in the box top (about one inch or two centimeters wide). This will allow light into your diorama. You can adjust the amount and type of light by what you put over this hole. Tissue paper can filter the light, for example.

5. Tape the top to the shoebox and decorate the outside of the box. Keep the decorations on the outside in line with the decorations on the inside.

Literature Discussion Group

Discussing what we read with others offers us a chance to share what we have learned, as well as consider the perspectives of group members. Working in literature discussion groups, you will discuss chapters 4–8 from *Bud, Not Buddy*. To prepare for your literature discussion, read chapters 4–8 and complete the questions on this page. Once you have completed this page, meet as a group to discuss your responses.

Write five questions that you can ask your group about chapters 4–8. Be sure to ask questions that will get others thinking about the book, as opposed to questions that can be answered with a simple "yes" or "no."

1. _____
2. _____
3. _____
4. _____
5. _____

Now select a character from *Bud, Not Buddy* that you think is most like you. Give a good explanation below, with examples, and be prepared to share with your group.

_____
_____
_____
_____

Select an event from the story and change the outcome. Some examples of events from the story could be when Bud is sent to a home, what happens at the Amoses, catching the train, meeting Deza Malone, etc. Be prepared to share your change of outcome with the group.

_____
_____
_____
_____

After meeting with your discussion group, answer the following questions on the back of this paper:

- ❍ How well did you listen to the other members of the group?
- ❍ Did you ask for clarification when you didn't understand a question?
- ❍ How well were you able to answer the questions? Have you done the reading?
- ❍ Did you participate in answering the questions of your group members?
- ❍ How can you improve as a member of a literature discussion group?
- ❍ How could your group improve as a literature discussion group?

Railroad Ties

Bugs and Bud try to catch a ride on the train heading west to pick fruit for pay. They were not alone. This was very common during the Depression. Thousands of men and boys were roaming America in search of a better life. Some left in search of employment; others left in shame over their family life being destroyed by the Depression; some left seeking adventure.

By the summer of 1932, it was very common to see hundreds of people hanging off the sides of train cars, as well as on the road. Most boys (and the occasional girl) traveled together in small groups, as it was a dangerous environment.

One of the most dangerous aspects of riding the rails was the train itself. Though it was thrilling to be riding at the top of the train across the Great Plains, it could also be deadly. Between the years of 1930 and 1939, it is estimated that approximately 24,000 people were killed and 27,000 were injured on railroad property.

However, riding the trains was not the only dangerous aspect of living on the road. There were multiple diseases transmitted, as well as poor conditions related to exposure, lack of cleanliness, and hunger. Most men and boys would go days without eating, and when they did eat, it was usually food left in the garbage, spoiled and unsanitary.

President Franklin D. Roosevelt enacted the Civilian Conservation Corps (CCC) to curb the amount of runaways and railroad trespassers. Unemployed and unmarried men between the ages of 18 to 25 were eligible to enroll. They were to be paid approximately $30 a month with most of those wages going to their families. These young men were put to work in national forests and parks. The CCC did not eliminate all of the runaways, as the permanent jobs did not come until after World War II began.

Questions to Consider

Use complete sentences to answer the following questions.

1. During the Depression, why did young men and boys leave home? _____

   _____

2. What were some of the dangers faced by these young men and boys riding the rails and walking the streets? _____

   _____

3. What was the CCC? What was its goal? _____

   _____

4. Are there still people on the streets today? Why? What do you think they are doing? _____

   _____

Extension: Watch the documentary *Riding the Rails*, which portrays the dilemma and life of the young men or boys riding the rails during the Depression. (See Bibliography for information.)

Compare/Contrast 1930s to Today

There are many differences between the way that you live and the way that Bud lived. Bud lived in a time more than 70 years ago. Just what has changed since then? Make a comparison between the way things are today and the way things were during the Depression. Use *Bud, Not Buddy* as a reference, as well as other books and resources available to you about the Depression. When you are finished, use the back of this paper to write down how you think things will change 70 years from now.

	1930s/Depression	Today
Entertainment		
Family Life		
Transportation		
Technology/ Communication		
Education		
Clothing		
Food		

Quiz Time

Answer the following questions about *Bud, Not Buddy*.

1. On the back of this paper, write a one-paragraph summary of chapters 9–11. Then complete the rest of the questions on this page.

2. How long will it take Bud to walk to Grand Rapids? _____

   _____

3. What could happen to a young black boy walking the Michigan streets in the middle of the night during the 1930s? _____

   _____

   _____

4. What does Bud do as soon as he gets inside the car? _____

   _____

5. What food does Mr. Lewis bribe Bud with to get in his car? _____

   _____

6. Why did Bud think that Mr. Lewis was a vampire? What was the blood for? _____

   _____

   _____

7. Who feeds Bud breakfast in the morning? Who are Scott and Kim? _____

   _____

   _____

8. What is a redcap? What is a Pullman porter? _____

   _____

   _____

   _____

9. Why does Mrs. Sleet "whop" her dad, Lefty Lewis, on the head with a wooden spoon? _____

   _____

   _____

10. What kind of seed does Bud compare to his idea of finding his father? _____

    _____

Stained Art Scenery

Use colored tissue paper and black construction paper to recreate a scene from the book. When finished and placed in the window, the paper has the same effect as stained glass.

Materials

- colored tissue paper
- black construction paper
- glue sticks
- pencils
- scissors
- drawing paper

Directions

1. Draw a simple design of a scene from *Bud, Not Buddy* on a piece of drawing paper. Do not overlap any of the objects in the scene. The designs need to be very simple. Next, cut out the simple designs.

2. Take the designs and objects cut from the scene, and place them onto the black construction paper. Trace around the outline.

3. Now, carefully cut out the designs from the black construction paper. Be careful not to cut the black area separating the designs.

4. Select the colors of tissue paper that you would like to work with. Remember to use a variety of colors.

5. Flip the construction paper so that it is on the back side. Place glue around each design and carefully paste down the tissue paper. Each piece and each color should be glued down individually.

6. When completed, the stained-glass art can then be placed on the window glass for display.

◆   ◆   ◆   ◆   ◆

Now write a poem to accompany your scene. Fill in the lines of the diamonte poem below, describing the stained-glass scene you have just made.

_____

title of stained art scenery (*1 word*)

_____

description of scene (*2 words*)

_____

action about the scene (*3 words*)

_____

feeling about the scene (*4 words*)

_____

synonym for the title (*1 word*)

Dicey Descriptions

On the back of this paper, draw a picture of Bud's suitcase. Then share your sketch with another student. Are the drawings similar? Why? They are similar because of the descriptive words that the author, Christopher Paul Curtis, used in *Bud, Not Buddy*. Descriptive words are adjectives. Mr. Curtis uses many descriptive words to help the reader visualize and imagine what is happening in the book.

What is an Adjective?

An *adjective* is a word that modifies, or changes, the meaning of a noun or pronoun. Here are some examples:

small, red schoolhouse   *big, tall* man   *soft, furry* puppy

---

Write a description, using adjectives, of each of the following nouns that you have read about so far in *Bud, Not Buddy*.

1. Bud's suitcase _____

2. the library _____

3. the Amoses' shed _____

4. Deza Malone _____

5. Bugs _____

6. Lefty Lewis _____

7. Hooverville _____

Circle the adjectives in the sentence below. Then rewrite the sentences and replace the adjectives with new ones. Think of synonymous adjectives that could replace the adjectives in the sentence.

1. The bright, yellow sun began to set on the horizon.

2. The big, dark clouds of dust were billowing from the north side of the farm.

3. The school books were ripped, torn, and filthy.

4. The long, tiresome line of people went around the mission twice.

5. His scrawny, skinny legs were poking out from under the covers.

Using Literary Devices

Authors use literary devices as tools when writing descriptive language. Read through the following literary devices and the examples of each.

Flashback—when the author takes the reader back to a time from the past and then takes the reader back to the present

Foreshadowing—when what is going to happen in the future is predicted or hinted about using words, imagery, or dialogue

Hyperbole—extreme exaggeration used to make a point or place emphasis

Onomatopoeia—words or phrases that sound like what they are describing, like the words hiss and bang

Rhetorical Question—when the author asks a question merely for effect with no answer expected

Simile—a word or phrase that compares one thing to another by using words such as *like* or *as*

Metaphor—a word or phrase that directly compares one thing to another

Find an example of each type of literary device described above in *Bud, Not Buddy*. An example has been done for you.

Literary Device	Example used in *Bud, Not Buddy*
Flashback	Bud begins checking his suitcase and pulls out the picture of his Momma on a horse. He remembers how she hated riding that horse and having her picture taken. He continues talking about her and the things she used to tell him. Then we read, "I checked out the other things in my suitcase and they seemed OK. I felt a lot better." (page 44)
Foreshadowing	
Hyperbole	
Onomatopoeia	
Rhetorical Question	
Simile	
Metaphor	

Rules to Live By

Bud creates a list of rules to live by. Each rule has a number, and each rule is "for having a better life and making a better liar out of yourself." Why do you think that Bud needs rules to have a better life? And why would he need rules to make a better liar out of himself? Listed below are some of the rules and things included in *Bud, Not Buddy*.

A fable is an imaginary story that intends to teach a lesson or a moral. With a partner, select one of Bud's rules and make up a fable for that rule. Use the rule as the moral to the story.

**Bud Caldwell's Rules and Things for Having a Funner Life
and Making a Better Liar Out of Yourself:**

Rules and Things #3

If you have to tell a lie, make sure it's simple and easy to remember.

Rules and Things #328

When you make up your mind to do something, hurry up and do it,
if you wait you might talk yourself out of what you wanted to do in the first place.

Rules and Things #83

If an adult tells you not to worry, and you weren't worried before,
you better hurry up and start 'cause you're already running late.

Now, write the rough draft of a fable, using a rule from your own life on the lines below. You may need to continue on another sheet of paper. When finished, read through your fable to check for spelling, grammar, and punctuation errors. Make a final draft of the fable to share with the rest of the class.

_____

_____

_____

_____

_____

_____

_____

_____

Extension: Read the fables together as a class. Locate the moral of the story. Then divide up into groups and act out the fables.

Quiz Time

Answer the following questions about *Bud, Not Buddy*.

1. On the back of this paper, write a one-paragraph summary of chapters 12–14. Then complete the rest of the questions on this page.

2. What was said on the telegram that Mr. Lewis sent? _____

    _____

    _____

3. What happened when Lefty and Bud were pulled over by the "copper"? _____

    _____

    _____

4. What did the flyer say that Lefty Lewis asked Bud to hide when the cop drove up? _____

    _____

5. What was Herman E. Calloway's reaction to Bud's claim that he was his son? _____

    _____

6. What was the name of the restaurant that was the first restaurant Bud had ever been to?

    _____

7. Who is Miss Thomas? How does she treat Bud? _____

    _____

8. What did Jimmy mean when he said Bud better be careful with his instrument because that was his "bread and butter in there"? _____

    _____

9. What are the names of the band members? _____

    _____

    _____

10. What did Bud start doing at the table in the restaurant? Why? _____

    _____

    _____

Home Movie History

The way we communicate has definitely changed over the years. Many of these new inventions have come about just in the last 20 years. Students will get a chance to research the history of communication and then make a home movie to share the results.

Materials

- small box (gelatin or pudding boxes work well)
- adding machine tape
- two pencils per students
- crayons or colored pencils
- aluminum foil
- tape

Directions

1. Assign each student the task of researching the history of communications, from the early 1900s to the present time. How have communication techniques changed? How was communication different for Bud than for children today? Make a time line on a piece of paper. Using the research, the students will then make a movie of the history of communication.

2. Ahead of time, cut a window in one side of a small, empty box for each student in your class. This hole needs to be the width of the adding machine tape.

3. Distribute the boxes to the students. Have students cover the boxes with aluminum foil and cut and fold the aluminum foil at the hole. Push the pencils through the sides of the box at the top and bottom. (You may wish to do this ahead of time for your students, as well.) See the illustration at the right.

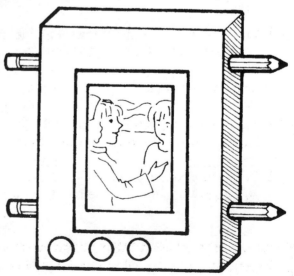

4. Distribute a section of the adding machine tape to each student. Students write words and color in each frame on the adding machine tape. Students draw illustrations to go with each invention. Tape the top of the adding machine tape to the top of the pencil. Then roll the pictures from top to bottom to create the "movies." Students read the story as they roll it and the illustrations through the box.

5. Divide students into groups of four or five. Allow time for each student to present their "movie." Have students discuss the inventions of communication and speculate on the future. How will things be different? Select the best movie to share with the class. Each group selects the best so the class will watch only four or five together.

Debating the Unions

Although labor unions did not begin during the 1930s, there were significant events and breakthroughs during this time period that brought labor unions to the forefront. We learn in *Bud, Not Buddy* that Lefty Lewis is involved in starting a union. We also learn that he was worried about the police officer finding out about his involvement with the labor unions. At this point in history, companies were threatening lockouts and blacklisting and pressuring workers from joining unions. Before the New Deal, employers could prevent employees from joining unions. When employees became free to join unions, it gave more power to the unions. Several key pieces of legislation and the New Deal programs dealt with the rights of workers and unions. A new type of strike, called a sit-down strike, was organized during the '30s and proved to be very beneficial. Research the NRA, NIRA, NLRA, and NLRB. Decipher the names of these organizations and determine how each helped workers.

You will be asked to debate the pros and cons of having a union. Determine whether you are for or against labor unions. Be prepared to back up your argument—pro or con—with factual information and data. Work through your argument, using the questions below.

○ What questions do you have about labor unions?

○ After your research, what have you learned about labor unions?

○ What are your opinions and feelings on labor unions? (The opinion statement begins with "I think" or "I believe." Example: *I believe that labor unions help keep things safe for the workers.*)

○ Write your thesis statement about labor unions. (This is not an opinion statement. Take the "I believe" or the "I think" part out of your opinion statement. What is left is the thesis statement. A thesis statement states a belief in an objective way. For example: *Labor unions help provide a safe environment for the workers.*)

○ List supporting details for your thesis statement. (Come up with at least three supportive statements that you have gathered from your research. These statements may include examples from personal experience, well-known facts, research, examples from text, expert opinion, or mathematical data.)

○ What is the opposing side going to say about your thesis statement? Have you anticipated what they will bring up to refute your argument?

○ List your counter-arguments. These are the things you will say to reinforce your claims and your argument.

Extension: Invite a labor union member to come and speak to your class about labor unions. Allow time for your students to ask questions. Next, invite a person from a large company that has a union to come and talk about the cons of having a labor union and what it does to a company.

The Telegraph and Morse Code

Since the beginning of time, people have been trying to communicate over long distances. After the discovery of electricity, wires were stretched from one point to another and an electric current was allowed to flow through the wires or broken by a switch called a telegraph key. The electric current was first used to make marks on a paper tape, and later it was used to make clicking sounds. The short and long times between the clicks could be decoded into numbers and letters from the alphabet.

This discovery allowed people to communicate instantly over large distances in ways that used to take days on horse or by train. Telegraph stations were first set up along the railroads because of the easy access of setting up poles along the tracks to hold the wires. At the beginning, the wires were used to communicate the movement of trains, and eventually the wires began to carry messages. In *Bud, Not Buddy*, Mr. Lewis sends a telegraph to Herman E. Calloway to let him know that Bud was on his way back home. Mr. Lewis explains to Bud that the shorter the message, the less expensive it is. Use International Morse Code to decipher the message below.

Letter	Morse		Letter	Morse		Number	Morse
A	• —		N	— •		0	— — — — —
B	— • • •		O	— — —		1	• — — — —
C	— • — •		P	• — — •		2	• • — — —
D	— • •		Q	— — • —		3	• • • — —
E	•		R	• — •		4	• • • • —
F	• • — •		S	• • •		5	• • • • •
G	— — •		T	—		6	— • • • •
H	• • • •		U	• • —		7	— — • • •
I	• •		V	• • • —		8	— — — • •
J	• — — —		W	• — —		9	— — — — •
K	— • —		X	— • • —			
L	• — • •		Y	— • — —			
M	— —		Z	— — • •			

• — • •   •   • • — •   —   — • — — / • •   • • • / • • — •   • • —   — •   — •   — • — —

___ ___ ___ ___   ___ ___ ___   ___ ___ ___ ___ ___

Now write your own message to a friend, using Morse code. (Remember to use the least amount of words possible.) Morse code must be typed in using "." for a dot and "-" for a dash. Letters have to be separated by spaces and words have to be separated by a slash.

Extension: Research on the Internet how to construct a telegraph. There are directions and diagrams to follow. Share your finished project with the class.

Euphemisms

A euphemism is the substitution of an agreeable or inoffensive expression for one that seems offensive or unpleasant. A euphemism is used to soften the meaning of a word. On page 178 in *Bud, Not Buddy*, Bud notices that the adults were using the word *gone* instead of saying that someone was dead. Other euphemisms for the word "dead" are *passed away*, *terminated*, or *bit the dust*. In the 1940s, the *Department of War* was renamed to be the *Department of Defense* because it seemed less offensive. What words do we use in our daily life to avoid saying something that might be offensive or suggests something unpleasant? Write the word(s) that has been replaced with the euphemism listed in the boxes. The first one has been done for you.

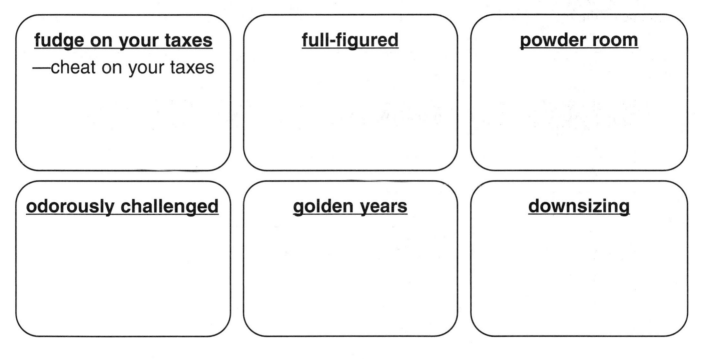

fudge on your taxes —cheat on your taxes	**full-figured**	**powder room**
odorously challenged	**golden years**	**downsizing**

Now write a euphemism for the simple, but sometimes unpleasant words or phrases below:

flunked	**vomit**	**came in last**

Extension:

- Watch political advertisements and locate examples of euphemisms being used by politicians or public leaders to "paint a pretty picture" of what they promise to do.
- Make a list of euphemisms that you hear your teacher and classmates using. You will be surprised how often euphemisms are used!

Quiz Time

Answer the following questions about *Bud, Not Buddy*.

1. On the back of this paper, write a one-paragraph summary of chapters 15–19. Then complete the rest of the questions on this page.

2. Where is the first city that Bud traveled with the band to?_____

_____

3. Why does Mr. Calloway keep a white person as a member of the band? _____

_____

_____

4. Why does Mr. Calloway collect rocks? What does he write on them? _____

_____

_____

_____

5. Is Herman E. Calloway Bud's father? What is he to Bud? _____

_____

6. What was Mr. Calloway's reaction when he found out about his daughter? _____

_____

_____

7. What instrument did the band members buy for Bud? _____

8. What is Bud's mother's name? _____

9. In whose room has Bud been sleeping? _____

10. What is the one thing that Bud saves to remember his mother by? Why do you think he chooses to save this item? _____

_____

_____

_____

All That Jazz!

At the end of the story, the band members buy Bud an alto saxophone. They expect him to learn to play so he can become part of the band. Imagine how exciting this would be for Bud! In the space below, design a jazzy poster advertising Bud's opening night. Next, transfer your work to a poster board. Select the tools (colored pencils, watercolor paints, crayons, or markers) you will use on your poster. Be sure to include a title for your poster.

On the Road Again

Herman E. Calloway and his band travel all over the place, earning a living by playing their music. Bud's mother used to ask her daddy to bring her home a "wock" from each of these places. Bud has a few of them, and discovers that Mr. Calloway's dashboard is full of them. These aren't just any ordinary rocks. They have words and numbers on them. For example, one reads: preston in. 6.4.36. Bud discovers that the words and numbers on the rocks represent places and dates of where and when Herman E. Calloway's band has traveled.

Using the map below, locate the following real places that the imaginary Dusky Devastators of the Depression traveled. Place the letter next to each city in the box on its corresponding line on the map.

A. Flint, Michigan	**D. Loogootee, Indiana**	**G. Idlewild, Michigan**
B. Gary, Indiana	**E. Chicago, Illinois**	**H. Sturgis, Michigan**
C. Kentland, Indiana	**F. Mecosta, Michigan**	

Labor Union Membership

Labor unions were placed in the spotlight again in the 1930s. In fact, many workers went on strike during this decade, including the California tree pruners, Briggs Manufacturing, Detroit Tool and Die, Hormel Meat Packing, the New Mexico miners, and the textile workers. Sit-down strikes became prevalent as well during the Depression, as workers attempted to keep their jobs during a strike. By 1938, Congress passed the Fair Labor Standards Act, which established the 40-hour work-week and the minimum wage and banned child labor in interstate commerce. That same year, the Congress of Industrial Organization (CIO) was founded with John Lewis as president. Union membership peaked in the 1950s and has been declining ever since. Though membership has declined in recent years, unions continue to be part of the labor force. Use the graph on union membership to answer the questions below.

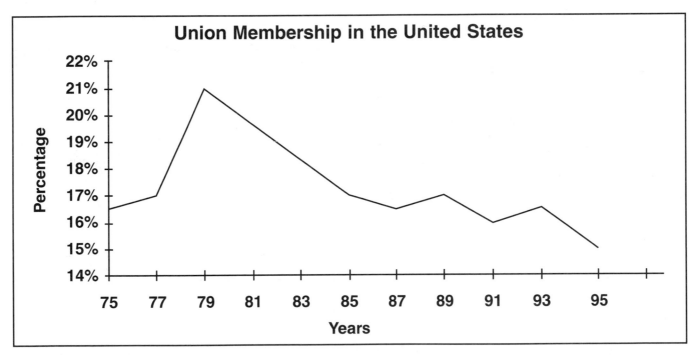

1. What was the percentage of union membership in the United States in 1991?

   _____

2. Why do you think membership dramatically increased in 1979?

   _____

3. What is the average percentage of membership for the years shown on the graph?

   _____

4. Approximately what percentage of workers were members of a union in 1975? 1985? 1995? What do you notice about the membership level in each of these decades?

   _____

5. Use the information from the graph above to create a bar graph on a separate piece of paper. In your opinion, which graph best displays the information?

   _____

Writing Historical Fiction

Sprinkled throughout *Bud, Not Buddy*, we find evidence of when the story takes place: during the Depression. This type of writing is called *historical fiction*. It is based on a real time period from history, but most, if not all, of the characters and plot are fictional. List examples from the story that show it took place during the Depression. The first one has been done for you.

1. In chapter 1, Bud talks about a flyer advertising the Dusky Devastators of the Depression. He mentions the year that his mother got the flyer being 1932 and that she has been dead for four years.

2. _____

 _____

3. _____

 _____

4. _____

 _____

5. _____

 _____

You will be asked to write an historical fiction story. Select a time period in history in which your book will take place. Do not include more than a 10-year span in your story, or it will become confusing and overwhelming. List five events that happened during the time period you have selected. You may need to check in an encyclopedia or history book to verify when these events happened.

1. _____

2. _____

3. _____

4. _____

5. _____

We also learn in the afterword of the book that the characters Lefty Lewis and Herman E. Calloway were based on Christopher Paul Curtis' grandfathers. When using people from real life, you do not necessarily need to use their real names, as Mr. Curtis did. The names can be changed. For the historical fiction story you are writing, base five of the characters on people from your life. They may be family members, friends, or acquaintances. List the real people from your life and then describe them, becoming familiar with them as characters. Then, decide on the name of the character.

People from your Life	Description	Name in the Story

Now you are ready to write the rough draft of your historical fiction story. Write the rough draft on the back of this paper or on another sheet of paper. Use the writing process to complete your story.

Famous Faces of the 1930s

Sprinkled throughout *Bud, Not Buddy* are references to famous and notorious people from the first part of the century. Just who are these people? Research and gather information on these individuals. Write a short statement about each of these people and why they are remembered from that time period. The page number next to each name references where this name is mentioned in *Bud, Not Buddy*.

Reference	Name of Person	What are they famous for?
page 17	John Dillinger	
page 29	Paul Robeson	
page 35	J. Edgar Hoover	
page 37	Pretty Boy Floyd	
page 37	The Real McCoy	
page 106	Baby Face Nelson	
page 112	Dorothy Dandridge	
page 133	Machine Gun Kelly	
page 136	Al Capone	
page 145	Jordan Snaggletooth MacNevin	
page 164	Blind Lemon Jefferson	

Now select one of the following activities to complete on one of the famous names above:

○ Research a person and write a report about him or her. How did he or she influence others? What is he or she known for in history?

○ Make a 'wanted' poster for this person, advertising his or her strengths or weaknesses. What is he or she wanted for?

○ Make a time line of this person and the things he or she accomplished in his or her life. Draw small illustrations to accompany each event on the time line.

○ Make a list of interview questions to ask this person. Research the answers that this person might have given to the questions.

○ Write and perform a play about the life of this person. Enlist the help of classmates to perform the skit. Use of makeup and costumes can enhance the performance. What other people need to be included?

Extension: Who are the faces of today? Who will be remembered in years to come? What are they famous for? Make a list of people that you think should be on a list. Who should not be included on the list? What do you think is the criteria for people to get on the list? Work as a class to come up with a top 10 list of famous people for our day.

Book Report Ideas

There are numerous ways to report on a book. After you have finished *Bud, Not Buddy*, choose one of the book report ideas to complete. You may also choose to design a book report of your choice, as long as it has been approved by your teacher. Be prepared to share your book report with the class.

1. Create a map showing where Bud's story takes place. Include a legend that describes what can be found on the map. The map can be colored on paper, or it can be done in 3-D.

2. Create an imaginary interview with a character of your choice from the book. Come up with at least ten questions that you could ask. Think of how the character would respond to the questions. You may even ask the class members to answer the questions as though they were the character.

3. Deliver an oral presentation to the class about the book. Select five objects that have significance to the story. Place the objects in a bag. As you give your oral presentation, pull the objects out one at a time to use as props or visuals.

4. Pretend that you are a professional critic and write a review of *Bud, Not Buddy*. Some tips to writing a professional review include writing in the third person omniscient point of view, using the present tense, anticipating and addressing the concerns of the reader, and supporting your opinion with evidence and examples from the book. Look up online reviews of *Bud, Not Buddy* on the Internet and locate examples of well-written reviews. How does yours compare?

5. Make a videotape of your favorite part of the story. Have family members or friends play the parts of other characters in the story. Dress up and wear things that Bud and other characters from the story would have worn. This will require some practice and some skill at using the video camera. Show your finished video to the class.

6. Make a comic strip about an event from the story. Make very neat and clear illustrations that are easy to see. Remember to keep the pictures simple and not too detailed so that it is easy to see what is going on. Double check your punctuation and spelling in the written part of the comic strip.

7. Write a letter to a friend telling him or her all about *Bud, Not Buddy*. Explain why you liked the story and why you think it would be good for him or her to read it. What did you learn from the story?

8. Illustrate 10 pictures on pieces of construction paper of characters or scenes from the story. Staple them together to form a book. On the back of each page, write a paragraph detailing what the illustrations are about. Remember to list personality traits of the characters.

9. Create something new in the story! Add a new character, a new plot, a new setting, a new conflict, a new ending, or a new beginning. Share your new element with the class.

10. Create a game which uses the story for material. This can be a board game or done in game-show format. Think up questions to be asked of the players of the game, with answers available. Do a practice run on your game and play it with a friend or family member to ensure that it runs smoothly. Talk to your teacher about scheduling a time to play the game with students in your class.

Letter to Christopher Paul Curtis

Use the business letter format below to write a letter to Christopher Paul Curtis. Once you have proofread the letter, you can then word process it on a computer. Check the letter for proper grammar, punctuation, and spelling. Create and design letterhead on which to print your letter. Display the letters on a bulletin board in your classroom.

_____
(first and last name of the sender)

_____
(address of the sender)

_____
(city, state abrreviation, and zip code of senders)

_____
(date the letter has been sent—don't use abbreviation for the month of the year)

_____
(first and last name of the recipient)

_____
(address of the recipient)

_____
(city, state abbreviation, and zip code of recipient)

Dear Mr. Curtis:

_____

_____

_____

_____

_____

_____

_____

_____

_____

Sincerely, (or other closing)

_____
(handwritten signature of the sender)

Thoughts and Themes

There are many themes found in *Bud, Not Buddy*. Some of these themes are friendship, sense of humor, racism, family relationships, hope, and survival. For each theme listed, there are activities, questions, and a suggested book related to that theme. Once you have answered the questions and read the book, or another book on that theme, select at least one activity to complete for each theme. Be sure to get approval from your teacher before beginning the activity.

Friendship

Questions about Friendship

- Who are Bud's friends? How can you tell?
- Who is not a friend to Bud? How can you tell?
- Is Herman E. Calloway a friend of Bud's?
- Why does everyone need friends?
- What does friendship bring to your life?

Book on Friendship

Paterson, Katherine. *Bridge to Terebithia.* Harper Trophy, 1997.

Friendship Activities

- Cut out from magazines pictures that portray friendship. Glue all of these pictures to make a friendship collage.
- Make a list of at least 10 qualities that you need to be a good friend.
- Write a letter to one of your friends telling them what their friendship means to you.
- Discuss the meaning of friendship with friends and family members. Look the word up in the dictionary, then write your own definition of friendship.

Sense of Humor

Questions about Sense of Humor

- Does Bud have a sense of humor? List examples you can find.
- Does Christopher Paul Curtis, the author, have a sense of humor? List three examples that support your answers.
- Why is it important to have a sense of humor?
- What makes you laugh?

Book on Sense of Humor

Gantos, Jack. *Joey Pigza Loses Control.* Farrar Straus & Giroux, 2000.

Sense of Humor Activities

- Find an appropriate and funny joke to share with the class.
- Write an original joke based on a personal experience that you have had.
- Select a comedian to research. How did life experiences prepare him or her for a career in comedy?
- Discuss guidelines to remember when poking fun at others. Remember to maintain dignity of others at all times.

Thoughts and Themes *(cont.)*

Racism

Questions about Racism

- Is racism exhibited in *Bud, Not Buddy*? List examples from the book to support your answers.
- Is racism still prevalent today? How can you tell?
- Is there an improvement in race relations since the 1930s? What evidence do you see?
- How much of racism is taught by parents to their children?
- What do you do to prevent and stop racism?

Book on Racism

Spinelli, Jerry. *Maniac Magee*. Little Brown & Co., 2000.

Overcoming Racism Activities

- Research civil rights in the United States of America. How far have we come?
- Write a one-page report about the history of civil rights.
- Make a promise to stop friends from making racists comments or sharing racists jokes. One can make a difference.
- Write a biography of Martin Luther King, Jr. Be sure to use more than one source for your information.

Family Relationships

Questions about Family Relationships

- Bud does not have any family at the beginning of the story. Throughout the book, who plays the role of family members for Bud?
- What was Bud's relationship like with his mother?
- Despite being related by blood, family relationships can still be strained. What do you think Bud's relationship will be like with Herman E. Calloway now that he knows Bud is his grandson?
- What are your family relationships like? Do you get along with members of your immediate family?
- Why are strong family relationships important?

Books on Family Relationships

Fox, Paula. *Monkey Island*. Yearling Books, 1993.

Cooney, Caroline B. *The Face on the Milk Carton*. Econo-Clad, 1999.

Family Relationship Activities

- Spend time with a family member that you haven't talked with much lately. Go on a "date" with that family member.
- Write secret notes to family members thanking them for their support and their love.
- Draw a family tree with as many names of your extended family as you can. What do you know about your ancestors? How have they affected your life?
- Send a video card to a family member that lives far away. Have someone videotape you.

Thoughts and Themes *(cont.)*

═══ Hope ═══

Questions about Hope

- How does having hope help Bud in his life?
- What are some examples of Bud having hope?
- Why is it important to have hope?
- Share a time when having hope made a difference to you.
- How do the flyers in Bud's suitcase represent hope?

Book on Hope

Snyder, Zilpha Keatley. *Gib Rides Home.* Delacorte Press, 1998.

Hope Activities

- Write and illustrate a book for young children encouraging them to have hope. Bind the book and make an appointment to read it to a first or second grade class. Talk with them about the importance of having hope in life. You may share personal examples in your story.
- Research and write a paragraph about 10 people that have exemplified hope. What struggle were they dealing with? How did hope help them overcome their struggles?
- Make a hope mobile. Draw pictures that represent hope and/or cut pictures from magazines. Hang the pictures from a hanger.
- Write a note of encouragement to someone who you know needs hope. Perhaps there is someone you know who is ill, just lost a family member, going through a divorce, etc. Offer words of hope.

═══ Survival ═══

Questions about Survival

- How is Bud a survivor? What type of survival skills does Bud use?
- How do the rules represent survival for Bud? Will he still need to use his "rules" with his new family?
- What survival skills have you learned in your life?

Books on Survival

De Young, C. Coco. *A Letter to Mrs. Roosevelt.* Delacorte Press, 1999.

Hesse, Karen. *Out of the Dust.* Scholastic Paperbacks, 1999.

Survival Activities

- Enlist the help of classmates and write a skit about survival. Work together to create the setting, the characters, the plot, the climax, and the ending.
- Living through the Depression was an act of survival in and of itself. Interview family members or neighbors that lived during the Depression and ask them about the survival skills needed to make it during that time. Record the conversation to share with the class. Be sure to begin the interview prepared with questions.
- Watch a video about the Depression. (See Bibliography for suggestions.) Write a review of the movie and compare the lives of those in the movie to Bud's life and to yours.

Books of the Depression

There are many books that—like *Bud, Not Buddy*—are written about the Depression. Select one or more of the following books to read. Locate them in your local or school library. Use the graphic organizer on page 42 to analyze and compare and contrast the book you read with *Bud, Not Buddy*.

Book List

Cochrane, Patricia A. *Purely Rosie Pearl.* Bantam Books, 1997.

Defelice, Cynthia C. *Nowhere to Call Home.* Farrar Straus & Giroux, 1999.

De Young, C. Coco. *A Letter to Mrs. Roosevelt.* Delacorte Press, 1999.

Ducey, Jean Sparks. *The Bittersweet Time.* Wm. B. Eeedrmans Publishing Co., 1995.

Hamilton, Virginia. *Drylongso.* Harcourt Brace, 1997.

Hesse, Karen. *Out of the Dust.* Scholastic Trade, 1997.

Koller, Jackie French. *Nothing to Fear.* Harcourt Brace, 1993.

Myers, Anna. *Red-Dirt Jessie.* Puffin, 1997.

Porter, Tracy. *Treasures in the Dust.* HarperCollins, 1997.

Raven, Margot. *Angels in the Dust.* Bridgewater, 1997.

Recorvits, Helen. *Goodbye Walter Malinski.* Frances Foster Books, 1999.

Taylor, Mildred. *Song of the Trees.* Laureleaf, 1996.

Thesman, Jean. *The Storyteller's Daughter.* Houghton Mifflin, 1997.

Willis, Patricia. *The Barn Burner.* Houghton Mifflin, 2000.

After you have completed your analysis of *Bud, Not Buddy* and the Depression book you selected, meet with someone who selected a different Depression book to read. Prepare ahead of time what you will say to your partner to encourage them to read your book. What did you like about the book? What did you learn about the Depression from this book? Why do you think your partner will enjoy reading this book? Meet with your partner and take turns discussing each book, including how the two books are similar and different.

Extension: Look up the online reviews of the books listed above. Which books have received awards? What makes an award-winning book stand out above the rest of the books?

Analyze This!

Use the graphic organizer below to analyze the book about the Depression that you read and compare and contrast it with *Bud, Not Buddy*.

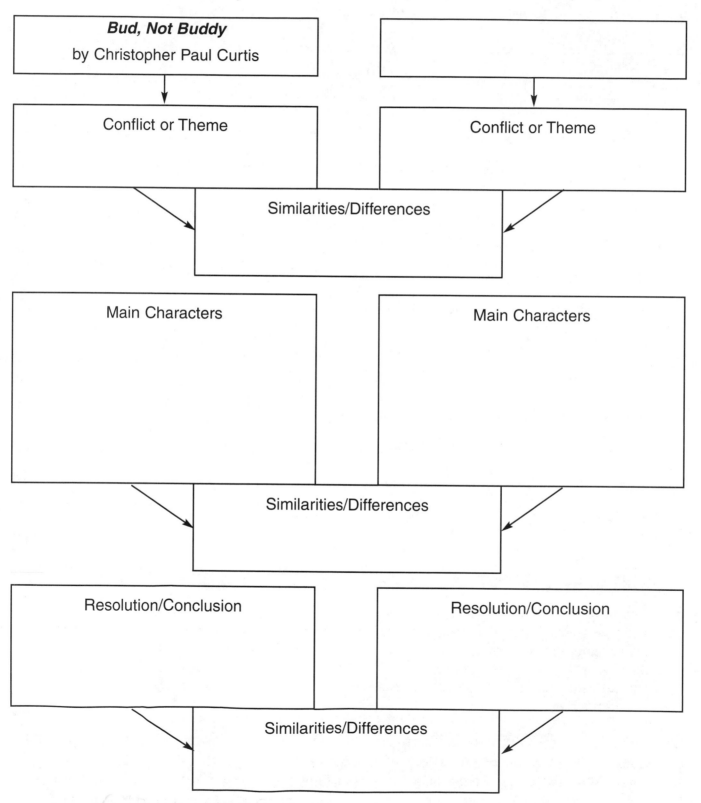

Unit Test

Matching: Match the descriptions with the correct people.

Mr. Sleepy LaBone	Miss Thomas	Deza
Lefty Lewis	Herman E. Calloway	Mrs. Sleet

1. _____ is "the most beautiful woman in the world."

2. _____ is the first girl Bud ever kissed.

3. _____ feeds Bud sausages for the first time.

4. _____ is orphaned at the age of six.

5. _____ sends a telegraph to Bud's "father."

6. _____ is the lead member of the jazz band

True or False: Write **true** or **false** next to the statement below.

_____ 1. Bugs shoves a pencil up Bud's nose.

_____ 2. Bud was never able to catch the train.

_____ 3. Lefty Lewis is arrested for his involvement with the Labor Unions.

_____ 4. Bud thinks that Miss Thomas is amazing.

_____ 5. The Amos family turns out to be a great foster family.

Short Answer: Use complete sentences to answer these questions.

1. How does Bud feel about his mother? _____

   _____

2. What instrument does Bud learn to play? _____

3. How does Lefty Lewis convince Bud to get in the car? _____

   _____

4. Why is Bud crying the night he ate dinner at a restaurant with the jazz band? _____

   _____

5. How does Bud get the nickname Mr. Sleepy LaBone? _____

   _____

Essay: On the back of this paper, write short essay answers to these questions.

1. What are the survival skills that Bud uses to make it in his life? List at least three examples of skills that Bud uses to endure and overcome the setbacks in his life.

2. Describe the relationship between Bud's mom and Herman C. Calloway. Discuss ways that you could tell that Momma still loved her father. In what ways could each of them have made their relationship better?

Reflections

Explain the meaning of each of these quotations from *Bud, Not Buddy*.

Note to the teacher: Choose the appropriate number of quotations to which your students should respond.

1. "Jerry must've been thinking just as hard as I was 'cause neither one of us said nothing, we just sat close enough so that our shoulders were touching."

2. "There comes a time when you're losing a fight that it just doesn't make sense to keep on fighting. It's not that you're a quitter, it's just that you've got the sense to know when enough is enough."

3. "Lord knows I have been stung by my own people before. But take a good look at me because I am one person who is totally fed up with you and your ilk. I do not have time to put up with the foolishness of those members of our race who do not want to be uplifted."

4. "Each head had a wide-open mouth with a sharp set of pointy teeth and lips smiling back ready to bite. It felt like the shed was getting smaller and smaller and the little mouths were getting closer and closer."

5. "Man! I was on the lam. I was just like Public Enemy Number One. If J. Edgar Hoover and the FBI saw me now I'd be in some real serious hot water."

6. "That's the part that gets the librarians the maddest, they get real upset if folks start drooling in the books, and page powder or not, they don't want to hear excuses, you gotta get out."

7. "Right when I was ready to push the covers off of me and start running or stabbing, whoever it was that had been watching jumped right on top of me. I was as trapped as a roach under a dishrag."

8. "We slapped our hands together as hard as we could and got our slobs mixed up real good, then waved them in the air so they'd dry. Now it was official, I finally had a brother!"

9. "I scooched my lips up and mashed my face on Deza Malone's. We stuck like that for a hot second, but it felt like a long time."

10. "I jumped in and out of Flint around seven times before that got boring and I decided I'd better head for Grand Rapids."

11. "The idea that had started as a teeny-weeny seed in a suitcase was now a mighty maple."

12. "Well, Bud, I don't mean to sully your reputation, but you just ran away from that man all the way across the state, I think I better hand-deliver you."

13. "Shucks. Finally I had to put my face in my arms on top of the table and put the napkin over my head. . . . It didn't look like I was gonna get this doggone valve closed any time soon."

14. "Shucks, as good as things were going for me now I'd bet you dollars to donuts that Steady Eddie was going to get here early."

Conversations

Work in size-appropriate groups to write and perform the conversations that might have occurred in each of the following situations.

○ Bud talks to Jerry about their new foster home assignments. (2 persons)

○ Bud talks to the librarian about what happened to Miss Hill. (2 persons)

○ Bud's pretend parents help him get in line for breakfast at the Mission. (4 persons)

○ Bugs talks to Bud, trying to get him to ride the rails with him. (2 persons)

○ Deza and Bud wash dishes together and talk about how people live on inside of us. (2 persons)

○ Mr. Lewis tries to convince and bribe Bud with food to get Bud into the car. (2 persons)

○ Bud eats breakfast with Mr. Lewis' daughter and her two kids. (5 persons)

○ Mr. Lewis and Bud are pulled over by a police officer worried about labor unions. (3 persons)

○ Bud tells Herman E. Calloway for the first time that he is his father. (2 persons)

○ The "Thug" teases Bud about pretending to be Calloway's son, and Steady Eddie sticking up for Bud. (3 persons)

○ Miss Thomas discusses the importance of not letting Mr. Calloway break Bud's spirit. (2 persons)

○ Bud rides with Mr. Calloway when Bud discovers that his rocks are just like the ones Mr. Calloway has in his car. (2 persons)

○ Mr. Jimmy and Miss Thomas talk with Bud when they find out the name of his mother. (3 persons)

○ Miss Thomas talks with Bud about how difficult it was for Mr. Calloway and the band members to learn that Bud's mother is dead. (2 persons)

○ Steady Eddie shows off the alto sax that he and the other band members bought for Bud. (2 persons)

Bibliography of Related Reading

Nonfiction

Brinkley, Alan. *American History: A Survey.* McGraw-Hill Inc., 1995.

Clark, Sarah Kartchner. *Literature Unit: Out of the Dust.* Teacher Created Materials, Inc., 1999.

———. *Thematic Unit: The Great Depression.* Teacher Created Materials, Inc., 1999.

The Depression. Golden Owl Publishing Co., Inc. 1972.

Filippelli, Ronald L. *Labor in the USA: A History.* Alfred A. Knopf, 1984.

Shebar, Sharon and Gary Lippincott. *Franklin D. Roosevelt & the New Deal.* Barrons Juveniles, 1987.

Uys, Errol Lincoln. *Riding the Rails: Teenagers on the Move During the Great Depression.* TV Book.

Videos

The Great Depression. PBS Video Films. 1320 Braddock Place, Alexandria, Virginia 22314, 1-800-424-7963.

Journey of Natty Gann. Walt Disney Films, 1997.

Riding the Rails. PBS Video. The American History Project/Out of the Blue Productions, Inc., 1-800-255-9424.

Web Sites

1930s and the Depression

http://www.cms.ccsd.k12.co.us/SONY/Intrecs/depwar.htm
http://newdeal.feri.org
http://www.nara.gov/exhall/newdeal/newdeal.html
http://www.research.att.com/history/train.html
http://www.mediahistory.com/time/1930s.html
http://www.amatecon.com/gdlinks.html
http://lcweb2.loc.gov/ammem/ndlpedu/timeline/depwwii/depress/hoovers.html

Christopher Paul Curtis

http://www.smplanet.com/bookclub/interactive/archive/curtis/curtisintro.html
http://www.powells.com/authors/curtis.html
http://www.randomhouse.com/teachers/authors/curt.html

Jazz

http://www.jazzhall.org/
http://www.allaboutjazz.com/timeline.htm
http://www.redhotjazz.com

Labor Unions

http://www.kentlaw.edu.ilhs/curricul.htm
http://www.sos.state.mi.us/history/museum/explore/museums/hismus/1900-75/depressn/laborun.html

Morse Code

http://www.soton.ac.uk/~scp93ch/morse/index.html

Newspapers

http://xroads.virginia.edu/g/1930s/print/printframe.html
http://www.nisk.k12.ny.us/fdr/ (editorial cartoons)
http://kailuahs.k12.hi.us/surfrider/ (an award-winning online student newspaper)

Answer Key

Page 10

2. He is sent to live with the Amos family.
3. Todd shoves a pencil up Bud's nose. Bud fights back, and Todd and Bud are hitting each other.
4. She is angry at Bud and feels sorry for Todd. She makes Bud apologize to Todd, and she sends Bud to sleep in the shed.
5. He is locked in the shed to sleep.
6. He thinks there is a vampire bat on the ceiling.
7. The vampire bat was really a nest of hornets. Bud is stung over and over again by hornets.
8. He breaks through the window and falls.
9. #3—If You Got to Tell a Lie, Make Sure It's Simple and Easy to Remember.
   #118—You Have to Give Adults Something That They think They Can Use to Hurt You by Taking It Away. That Way They Might Not Take Something Away That You really do Want. Unless They're Crazy or Real Stupid They Won't Take Everything Because if they Did they Wouldn't Have Anything to Hold Over Your Head to Hurt You with Later.
   #328—When You Make Up Your Mind to Do Something, Hurry Up and Do It, If You Wait You Might Talk Yourself Out of What You Wanted in the First Place.
10. The flyers advertise Herman E. Calloway and his jazz band performing in the local cities.

Page 13

1. 10 million
2. 15 square feet
3. 50 miles
4. 4 million
5. 900%
6. 20%
7. 10 million unemployed
8. 477 children
9. 45 pounds
10. 4,000 boys and 6,000 girls
11. 6/8 (or 3/4) of the vegetables
12. 1,500,000 people

Page 15

2. He clogged up their kitchen sink and turned the water on so that it would overflow. He also dipped Todd's hand in hot water and got him to wet the bed.
3. She got married and moved to Chicago, Illinois.
4. She didn't want to have her picture taken, ride on the poor miniature pony, or wear the filthy hat.
5. She liked to tell Bud about the picture she had taken on the miniature horse. She told him that when one door opens, another door closes. She also told him that he was named Bud, and not to let people call him Buddy. And finally, she would say, "Don't worry Bud, as soon as you get to be a young man I have a lot of things I'll explain to you."
6. A family pretended that Bud was in their family. He got brown sugar sprinkled on his oatmeal.
7. Deza is a girl that Bud met at the Hooverville outside of Flint. Deza is the first girl that Bud has ever kissed.
8. Hooperville was actually a Hooverville, which were little cardboard shack towns that sprung up during the Depression because people lost their homes. The towns were named after President Hoover, who was the president of the United States and was blamed for the economy.
9. He is not able to catch the train. As he threw his suitcase to Bugs, a flyer flew out. Bud slowed down to get the flyer, and the train went on too quickly.
10. They both have eight letters in them and start with a "C."

Page 20

2. It will take him 24 hours to walk.
3. A black person walking the streets that time of night could be hurt by anyone that was racist.

4. Bud tries to drive off and leave Mr. Lewis.
5. He bribes him with a bologna sandwich, an apple, and red pop.
6. He thinks Lefty is a vampire because he is carrying a cooler that has human blood in it. The blood is for the Hurley Hospital in Flint.
7. Mrs. Sleet, Mr. Lewis' daughter feeds Bud breakfast. Scott and Kim are Mr. Lewis' grandchildren.
8. A redcap is the person who takes people's bags to their train cars. A porter is the person who takes care of the people once they are on the trains.
9. She does it because Lefty keeps teasing her about her "paincakes" and her cooking.
10. He compares the idea to the seed of a maple tree.

Page 25

2. The telegram said "HEC STOP BUD OK IN FLINT STOP AT 4309 NORTH ST STOP RETURN 8 P.M. WED STOP LEFTY STOP."
3. The police officer looked in the trunk and in the back seat of the car. He also asked what was in the suitcase. He was stopping cars he didn't recognize, looking for labor organizers who might be sneaking up from Detroit.
4. The flyers were announcing and advertising an informational meeting for railroad workers to come and learn about the union branch being formed.
5. He seems angry. He thinks Bud is a disturbed young man and tells him to go back where he came from.
6. The name of the restaurant is The Sweet Pea.
7. Miss Thomas is the singer for the band. She is very kind and gentle with Bud.
8. He meant that he earned his money with the instrument that was inside the case.

Answer Key *(cont.)*

9. The band members are Mr. Jimmy, Doug "The Thug" Tennant, Steady Eddie Patrick, Chug "Doo-Doo Bug" Cross, Roy "Dirty Deed" Breed, Miss Thomas, and Herman E. Calloway.

10. He started crying. He was overcome with emotion. He was happy to be home, to have found his father, and to be around people that were so nice to him.

Page 28

Message: Lefty is funny.

Page 30

2. The first city Bud traveled with the band to was Mescota, Michigan.

3. He has the white person in the band to help set up engagements for the band because many people may not hire the band if they knew it was an all-black jazz band. Mr. Calloway also puts the house in the white member's name.

4. He collects the rocks because when his daughter was little she asked him to bring home a "wock." He writes the dates and the places where the band performs.

5. No, he isn't Bud's father. He is Bud's grandfather.

6. He was shocked. He went upstairs to cry.

7. The band members gave Bud an alto saxophone.

8. Her name is Angela Janet Caldwell (Calloway).

9. He has been sleeping in the room his mom had when she was a little girl.

10. He ends up keeping one rock on which is written Flint and the date the band played there.

Page 32

Page 33

1. 16%

2. Answers will vary.

3. Approximately 16%

4. About 16.5% in 1975, 17% in 1985, and 15% in 1994. The percentages remain about the same through each decade, although there is a slight increase and then decrease.

5. Answers may vary.

Page 35

John Dillinger: famous bank robber

Paul Robeson: contemporary singer and actor in 1930s

J. Edgar Hoover: former director of FBI

Pretty Boy Floyd: gangster of the 1930s—wanted by FBI

The Real McCoy: black inventor of over 57 devices

Baby Face Nelson: gangster and bank robber wanted by FBI

Dorothy Dandridge: famous black actress

Machine Gun Kelly: gangster and bank robber wanted by FBI

Al Capone: famous gangster from Chicago

Jordan Snaggletooth MacNevin: fighter out of Chicago

Blind Lemon Jefferson: popular blues recording artist

Page 43

Matching

1. Miss Thomas

2. Deza

3. Mrs. Sleet

4. Mr. Sleepy LaBone

5. Lefty Lewis

6. Herman E. Calloway

True/False

1. False

2. True

3. False

4. True

5. False

Short Answer

1. Bud loves his mother. He misses her. He remembers her well.

2. He learns to play the alto saxophone.

3. He bribes him with a bologna sandwich, red pop, and an apple.

4. He is overcome with emotion. He feels loved and that he is a part of something for the first time in his life. He feels safe.

5. "Sleepy" comes from the fact that he sleeps so much. "Bone" is because he is so skinny. The La part was added to bone because la bone is French. They wanted to show that Bud was classy.

Essay

Answers will vary.